Johnnie's Poems

FRONTISPIECE *Johnnie aged 8*

Johnnie's Poems

Poems and Other Pieces
Written in Childhood
by
Johnnie Douglas-Pennant

1987–2004

EDITED BY
SARAH DOUGLAS-PENNANT

The Anna Trust

© Sarah Douglas-Pennant

First published by The Anna Trust November 2005
Reprinted with an additional poem March 2006

ISBN 10 1 84529 433 5
ISBN 13 978 1 84529 433 5

Designed by Humphrey Stone
Printed by Salisbury Printing

Cystic Fibrosis is the UK's most common life-threatening disease
with around 7,000 children and adult sufferers. It is progressive, and affects
lungs and digestion, leading to chronic chest infections. Research is leading to
great improvements in treatment though there is still no cure.
The Anna Trust supports research beneficial to those
with well-developed CF and has so far contributed over £500,000
to research and equipment at Southampton University Hospital.

The Dyspraxia Foundation offers support and information on
dyspraxia. This book is sold in aid of both these causes.

To obtain further copies please write to Peta Nightingale
32 Holly Grove, London SE 15 5DF, enclosing a cheque, made out
to The Anna Trust, for £12.50 to include postage.

Contents

Foreword

When our beloved son Johnnie died tragically in a swimming accident last summer at the age of seventeen, we were left with a huge wave of emotion from his and our friends, and a collection of his poems and other writings which I had kept and treasured for years. The wave of emotion eventually transformed itself into a walk in his memory by his family and many of his friends. This took place in July and August the following summer, covering 600 miles from Southampton Football Stadium, (he was a great Saints supporter) to the Isle of Jura in the Hebrides, where we had spent a fortnight every summer of Johnnie's life. We made this pilgrimage carrying his ashes, with friends of all ages taking part along the way. In addition, Johnnie's Walk raised in excess of £200,000 for research into cystic fibrosis. We decided that the poems and other funny pieces he had written should be shared with a wider audience . To this end I have edited them into this book, to be sold in aid of The Anna Trust for cystic fibrosis research, founded in 1993 in memory of Johnnie's sister Anna, with a percentage going also to the Dyspraxia Foundation.

There is a box of treasures in our house, a whole legacy of memories from all our three children tucked away. In it there are keepsakes reflecting the character and abilities of each child. Anna, seven years Johnnie's senior, was pony-mad, and her cards often reflect a horsey theme. Hers is the beautiful handwriting done for a competition, the still life drawings, the letters begging to be allowed a pony, the furious notes pushed under the door in the heat of an angry moment, and the endearingly honest apologies. Milly, a year and a half younger and the

7

most artistic of the three, has made lovingly crafted missives bordered with little flowers, and later wonderful work-of-art cards of all kinds. Her school books are filled with beautiful writing and pictures. They all made home-made birthday cards, drawings, funny letters and pictures. Johnnie was not creative like his sisters when it came to making cards. What he did produce was an assemblage of poems. I had kept them carefully, knowing that these things come once in a childhood and then the moment passes, never to return. They now have an added poignancy and it has been a wonderful task of closeness to Johnnie to prepare them for the book, bringing a vivid sense of his presence as his words and humour have come alive again on the page.

Among those who have helped with this book, I would like in particular to thank Amanda Vesey, Pen Milburn and Humphrey Stone who have all given a great deal of time to help make sure we did the contents justice, and have lent the project much invaluable support and encouragement.

SARAH DOUGLAS-PENNANT
7 February 2006

Poems

The Angry Sea

Johnnie Douglas-Pennant was born on the 5th May 1987. His two elder sisters, then aged six and seven, had both been born with cystic fibrosis but he was healthy and clear. The whole family were completely delighted by the new member of the family and he had an instant doting fan club from his sisters and from their friends. He was the merriest of tots, with a gloriously infectious laugh, easy with everyone but also happy to play for long periods by himself. He grew into an enchanting, lively, imaginative small boy, interested in all sorts of things that captured the imagination, such as history and legends, myths and bible stories.

When he was six his fourteen year-old elder sister Anna died of complications of CF. This was a terrible blow to Johnnie who adored his sisters and had loved Anna ever more tenderly as she grew iller and weaker. At the same time he was discovering that school work was a struggle owing to his still undetected dyspraxia, which meant he was poorly co-ordinated and had dyslexic type difficulties with reading and writing. He was being left behind in school work by his peers who one by one moved up into the next class while he remained behind. Six months after Anna died we moved him to a new school.

Johnnie started at Port Regis School in the summer term at just seven, and in the September he was fortunate in finding himself with an inspirational teacher, Mrs Staniforth. He arrived in her class still barely able to spell or write legibly. One day when I went to collect him from school she called me over. 'Look at this,' she said, handing me Johnnie's writing book. They had been doing Poetry that afternoon, and had been encouraged to write some themselves. Written in pencil on an untidy page was the poem that follows, which is what Johnnie had astonished her by producing:

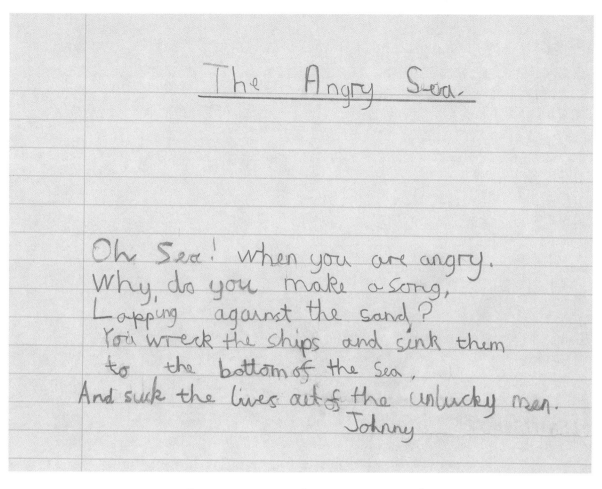

The Angry Sea.

Oh Sea! when you are angry.
Why, do you make a song,
Lapping against the sand?
You wreck the ships and sink them
to the bottom of the sea,
And suck the lives out of the unlucky men.

Johnny

First version 4 February 1995 aged 7

Mrs Staniforth was so delighted with the poem that she made him write it out in his very best handwriting (illustrated above) and sent it to the headmaster. He wrote underneath it: 'This is an excellent piece of work Johnnie. The last line reminds me of Homer, a Greek poet who lived about 2700 years ago and who is thought to be the greatest poet ever! Well done!'

The discovery that he could write poetry was a revelation to us all, not least to Johnnie himself. He had had the great good fortune to have realised a talent which could easily have lain unsuspected indefinitely. Now he had something which might lift him from the ignominy of the bottom of the class. Fired up, there followed a period of great writing activity, the results of which are published here. He continued to write poems on occasion throughout his life after this, though never again at quite such a rate. Unfortunately that first school book has been lost but Johnnie wrote this poem out again for various people and in slightly dif-fering versions, and the originals of these remain.

For example, a few days later he did one illustrated with a picture of a ship, as depicted opposite, whose name when deciphered from the mirror writing reads 'The Happy and glorious':

Sea

Oh! Sea when you are angry, why do you
make a song, lapping Against the beach and
Singking the ships to the bottom of sea or wrecking
Them and sucking the lives out of The unlucky
men?

NOTE TO READER
Johnnie's words have been set in large type exactly as he wrote them, where necessary adding a translation in smaller type. In a few cases where it seemed appropriate, they have been set out as a poem.

Sea

Oh! Sea when you are angry, why do you
macke a song, lapping against the beach and
Singking the ships to the bottom of Sea or wrecking
Them and sucking the lives out of The unlucky
men?

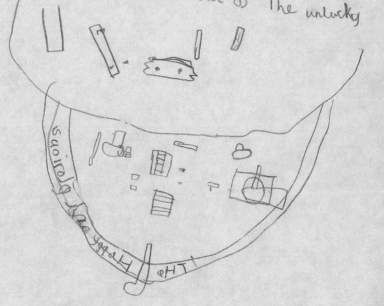

After this, it was as if a door had been opened and over the next days and weeks Johnnie wrote poems whenever inspiration struck, at home, in the car, in bed before going to sleep, and also at school.

The Sky

the sky it cares wundfull things like
the sturs and the sun. It macks a plas
for the berds to fliye fry. And a plas for
us gase up at. I dont no wot we wood of
dun with out the sky.

12 February 1995 aged 7

TRANSLATION

The Sky

The sky it carries wonderful things
Like the stars and the sun.
It makes a place for the birds to fly free.
And a place for us to gaze up at.
I don't know what we would have
Done without the sky

The Sky

the sky it cares wundfull things like
the stars and the sun It macks a plas
for the berds to fliye fry And a plas for
trs gase up at I dont no wot we wood us
dun with out the sky.

The Night

As darkners creeps over theis side of the world,
And the creatures come out to intoy the night,
Theay cum on the baks of ouls and bats and
snayalls. To a purticklar big pleas. And theay
do wot ever vaye wont for ther is no wun adowt.

12 February 1995 aged 7

The Night

As darkness creeps over this side of the world,
And the creatures come out to enjoy the night,
They come on the backs of owls and bats and
snails. To a particular big place. And they
do whatever they want for there is no one about.

The Night

A2   darkriers creeps over   theis side of the world.
And the creatures come out to intoy the night
theay cum on the baks of ouls and bats and
spayolls. To a purticktar big pleas. And theay
do wot ever voye wont for ther is no wcn adowt.

The Sea

The sea is a byoterfoll thing its pure ocheans ur so blue
but behold it carries meny dangers like sharks
and sorms sending men into the salty wet
sea. In sun set the sea is so byterfoll that
no man can make any thing as wundfll

12 February 1995 aged 7

The Sea

The sea is a beautiful thing
Its pure oceans are so blue.

But behold it carries many dangers
Like sharks and storms
Sending men into the salty wet sea.

In sunset the sea is so beautiful that
No man can make any thing as wonderful.

The Sea

The sea is a byoterfoll thing its but behold it carries meny dangers like sharks ocheans ur so blue and sorms sinding men into the salty wet zea. In sun set the zea is so byderfoll theat no man can make any thing as wrundfll

The Oshon Batall

The batall ships gointo the line of enerme
the wall of def the fite bgings a canon fiyers
a must falls and the rithalls boing to fiyer
men foll into the sea and dive into the haches
for cuver from the rithall fiyere.

13 February 1995 aged 7

TRANSLATION SET AS A POEM

The Ocean Battle

The battle ships go into the line of enemy
The wall of death
The fight begins
A canon fires
A mast falls
And the rifles begin to fire.
Men fall into the sea
And dive into the hatches
For cover from the rifle fire.

The picture opposite was used as a Get Well Soon card for Milly

The Oshon batall

The batall ships goint the line of enerme
the wall of des the zite bging a conon figers
a must, folls and the rithalls boing to figen
men zoll into the sea and divets into the haches
for wver from the rithall figere.

get well zoom

The Sea

Oh how Sun glisons on the sea and mackes it look
as if the sea is a different sky for it has stars in it wen the
sun shines on the surface of the sea.

14 February 1995 aged 7

The Sea

O how the Sun glistens on the sea
And makes is look as if
The sea is a different sky,
For it has stars in it when the sun
Shines on the surface of the sea.

The Sea

Oh, how sun glisons on the sea, and mackes it look as if the sea is a different sky for it has stars in it, wen the sun shines on the surface of the sea.

The Sea

Oh hou the sea gliters in the sun lite of the erley
day. And as it laps aganst the rocks it makes a
song of its onn. A speshal and wunderfall song. No
myosishon (can) mach it

Written on a slip of paper folded up and addressed to DAD
February 1995 aged 7

The Sea

O how the sea glitters in the sunlight of the early day
As it laps against the rocks it makes a song of its own.
A special and wonderful song
No musician can match it

The Sea

oh hou the sea gliters in the sun late, of the erley
day And. Az it laqs agenst the rocks it makes a
song of its onn. A speshal and wrunder fall song no
myvoisbon can matchit

The Blasing Sun

How the sun blases big and red in the sky
oh sun stay for ever so I can look at you.
You ur the king of planits in the millkey way.
Yor hyoog bems ur yor crown. You ur wundfoll.

13 February 1995 aged 7

The Blazing Sun

How the sun blazes big and red in the sky
Oh sun stay for ever so I can look at you.
You are the king of the planets in the Milky Way
Your huge beams are your crown.
You are wonderful.

myosick
Anermo
Sun

THE Blasing Sun

How the sun blases big and red in the sky
oh sun stay for ever so I can look at you.
You ur the king of the planits of the millkey way.
Yor hyoog berns ur yor crown you ur wundeafl

Wording for Anna's bench

By the second anniversary of the death of Johnnie's elder sister Anna from cystic fibrosis, we were planning a bench in her memory, to be placed beside the river, and thinking what wording to have carved on it. Johnnie came up with an answer which we felt could not be bettered.

Anna Douglas-Pennant's ashes lie as a memory in this river
Died 2nd October 1993

OPPOSITE *Johnnie with Anna, aged 5 and 12, 1991*

By this time I had taken to going into the classroom to look at Johnnie's writing book before I collected him, and used to copy any new poems into my own notebook before they got lost.

Down in the Sea

Down under the sea out of mans reach.
There are empty dark dark caves. It is
so dark that even the brightest light
will shine very dimly. Thousands of
tiny shells lie on the sand. Only the biggest
fish go in but sometimes they don't come out.

Creative writing at school, the subject given: The Dark
25 February 1995 aged 7

Bulbs

As I lie in that soil a long glow worm comes by pulling light to me.
When I sprout I shall be a beautiful bluebell in the forest above me.
And when I sprout up into the air and light it shall be wonderful.
Ah, I can feel myself sprouting, but it shall be a long time until I
become a bluebell.

Creative writing at school
4 March 1995 aged 7

As the Sheet of Darkness

As the sheet of darkness is dropped
And the wolves start singing their songs
The owls come out to hunt
Mice run in despair
Voles hide
A spider's web hangs from the trees
A smell of fungus is around
And a breeze sends water dripping from the trees.

7 May 1995 just 8

*Dictated after walking 10 miles for the Save the Children
Fund Wessex Walk.*

MRS STANIFORTH

The next nine poems were written at school so it seems appropriate here to talk about Mrs Staniforth. She has finally retired now although until recently she still worked part time. She was the wonderful teacher who inspired Johnnie to write poems. She was well over seventy when she was teaching Johnnie, but more bright and active than someone half her age. She was truly dedicated and a born teacher. She had whispy white hair and dangly earrings and came to school every day on her bicycle. When I was assembling the material I rang her to ask her how she did it. She told me that she would read lots of poems to the class, would give them good descriptive pieces. She would get their imagination going and then let it go on from there.

'Johnnie was particularly sensitive,' she said. 'He was a wonderful pupil to teach'. She continued: 'I never read them trashy stuff. I used material which some people might have felt was too advanced but I didn't want to limit them. I wanted them to reach for the stars'. Whatever the subject set was, she would read descriptive pieces about it first.

'Poetry is a passion of mine. The magic of words. I wanted to pass on this enthusiasm. It's most important to build up the child's confidence, to make them feel that their work is as good as the next child's, to make them believe in themselves.'

The Deserted Beach

As the sea sings its song and
Sea stars shine
The sky goes red
The sea gulls chorus the song of the sea
Sails shine like fire
Some driftwood shaped
half dragon half bird

Creative writing at school
20 May 1995 aged 8

Lion

Se this Lion he has the stref of ten men he drops to the ground a buferlo chues the lion spings to the fest of meat he flicks his gors fratic his jous fratickle and cillis his pra and ets

School book 1995 aged 8

TRANSLATION

See this Lion. He has the strength of ten men. He drops to the ground. A buffalo charges. The lion springs to the feast of meat. He flicks his jaws frantic his jaws frantically and kills his prey and eats.

SET AS A POEM BY AUTHOR AND FRIEND
GEORGIE HAMMICK

Lion

See this lion
He has the strength of ten men
He drops to the ground.
A buffalo charges
The lion springs
to the feast of meat. He flicks his jaws
Frantically
And kills his prey
And eats.

Se this Lion he has the stres of ten
men her drops to the ground a
buferlo chuus the Lion spings
to the fest of met he flicks
his goos fratick his Jows fratickle
and cillis his pra and ets

The Old House

Oh how that ancient
house stans fall of dark
Blak secrets. With a door so
stif no mans hand can open it
I wish I could Now thos secrets.

17 July 1995 aged 8

A poet friend saw Johnnie's poems and was interested. We went to visit him in Winchester and he encouraged Johnnie to keep writing. Johnnie wrote the poem above for him.

TRANSLATION

The Old House

O how that ancient house
Stands full of dark black secrets
With a door so stiff no
man's hand can open it
I wish I could know those secrets

The OLD HOUSE

O'h how that ~~old~~ ancient
house stans sall of dark
Blak secrets. With a door so
stif no mens hand can open it
I wish I could Now thos secrets.

The Ocean

The Ocean is so Beaetiful
with its day stars.
But Behold when the sea gats
angry and makes a stom.
It swolows men and sucs ther
   lives out.

14 September 1995 aged 8

TRANSLATION

The Ocean

The ocean is so beautiful
With its day stars.
But behold when the sea gets
Angry and makes a storm
It swallows men
And sucks their lives out.

The Ocean is SO Beaetiful
with it's day stars.
But Behold when the Sea gats
angry and makes a Stom.
It Swolows men and sucs ther
Lives out.

The Oshon is so Beawtifly whith
it's day stus and Brockers

First try

The Seas Power

As I whoch that storm and lisn to the seas song. The dolfons darns to the fers song. But the sea derstrous ships on the rock's and sucs the livs out of the unlucky men. doun go the unlucky men to the reset hov ben atarkt by the sea and drownd

First page of a new book at school
October/November 1995 aged 8

TRANSLATION

As I watch that storm and listen to the sea's song, the dolphins dance to that fierce song. But the sea destroys ships on the rocks and sucks the lives out of the unlucky men. Down go the unlucky men to the rest who've been attacked by the sea and drowned.

Two versions opposite: first one only translated here.

The Seas Power

A2 I whoch that storm and lisn to the Seas song. The dolfons darnc to the fers song. But the Sea derstraus ships on the rock's and sucs the lus out of the unlucky men. doun go the unlucky men to the reset hov ben atarks by the Sea and drownd

A2 I whoch that stor and lison to the Seas song and whach the dolfins dans to that fers song. The sea vs desroing the ships on the robs and such the lives out of unlucky men. Down go thos men to Town the over men hour been atort by the Sea

A Walking in the Woods

Wen a went warking in the wood. All the birds were
singing One or two were eteing beres happerle.
The were quite alote of sting netalls and the twigs are
crunching. I like to wirk in the shadows of blak paches of
lite sneking. I kane hier the laping of a strem. I feall tard
but happy and warm.

Creative writing at school
7 November 1995 aged 8

A Walking in the Woods

When I went walking in the wood all the birds were singing. One or
two were eating berries happily. There were quite a lot of stinging
nettles and the twigs are crunching. I like to walk in the shadows of
black patches of light sneaking. I can hear the lapping of a stream. I
feel tired but happy and warm.

OPPOSITE *Johnnie and Milly aged 7 and 13. This was Johnnie just*
before he started writing the poems.

43

Christmas

Carol singers every ware.
Holly on evry dor
Red flames in the fier.
In all the houses is a Christmas three
Santer fills evryones stokings.
Tofy fug and all things nice.
Mases of minc piys
A palpiys all nice and wam

4 December 1995 aged 8

TRANSLATION

Christmas

Carol singers everywhere
Holly on every door
Red flames in the fire.
In all the houses is a Christmas tree
Santa fills everyone's stockings.
Toffee fudge and all things nice.
Masses of mince pies
Apple pies all nice and warm

Christmas

Carol singers every ware.
Holly on evry dor.
Red flams in the fier.
In all the houses b na christmas three
Santer fills evryones stokings.
Tofy fug and all things nice.
Mases of minc piys.
A palpiays all nice and wam

After the rain

After the rain evrything is fresh and beautiful. The flowers are sweetsmeling and are in full bloom. The birds are just starting to sing, a small brease is pushing the plants around. The puduls are shing in the sunlight. The sky is cloudy but the sun is just cuming out.

Creative writing at school
December 1995 aged 8

TRANSLATION

After the rain

After the rain everything is fresh and beautiful. The flowers are sweet-smelling and are in full bloom. The birds are just starting to sing. A small breeze is pushing the plants around. The puddles are shining in the sunlight. The sky is cloudy but the sun is just coming out.

Lots and Lots
of Love
mate

Painting done for Dad's birthday, 7 February 1996 aged 8

Winter

Oh seson of forsts and sonow. O killer of summer.
Oh maker of everthing so cold and white
Sending first Jack Frost panting evrething so white
With his pante brush. Then the snow cums berowing all
the flowers under its blanket.
Oh how ruff the winter is.

Johnnie listened to some people doing readings about winter and then wrote this poem.

11 December 1995 aged 8

Winter

O season of frosts and snow. O killer of summer.
O maker of everything so cold and white
Sending first Jack Frost painting everything so white
With his paint brush. Then the snow comes burying all
the flowers under its blanket.
O how rough the winter is.

Winter

Oh seson of foots and
snow. oh killer of
~~rtt~~ summer. oh maker of
everthing so cold and
white. Sending ferst Jack
Frost panting everthing
so ~~wight~~ white with ~~pishar~~
pante brush. Then the
snow ~~cum~~ cums berow
-ing all the flowers under
its ~~bllanket~~ bllanqket.
Oh how ~~ruff~~ the winter
is.

White

Wite is a seagull
And a wating felling
A pare of traneres in a shop
A dirty ballkbord to
Wites a new soot shert
It's a cloud drifting
Acros the sky
And it's the page of a Book
It's the couler of forling

School book 17th January 1996 aged 8

White

White is a seagull
And a waiting feeling
A pair of trainers in a shop
A dirty blackboard too
White's a new suit shirt
It's a cloud drifting
Across the sky
And it's the page of a book
It's the colour of falling

WHITE

Wite is a seagull
Anda wating felling
A pare of traneres in a shop
A dirty ballkbord to.
Witres a new soot shert
Its a cloud drifting
Acros the sky
And its the page of a Book
Its the couler of forling

by _Johnnie Douglas-_

Football

Monty Keith Jim George Barry Dave Mark Andy Neil Julian

Evens United get picked for the FA cup but one of their players gets hurt so a player who doesn't know how to do proper shots comes on.

Evens United get into the 5th round of the FA Cup and win 4-2.

Evens United get into the semi-final of the FA Cup and first of all they draw 1-1, then they win 2-0 and then they win the Final 3-2

School book aged 8

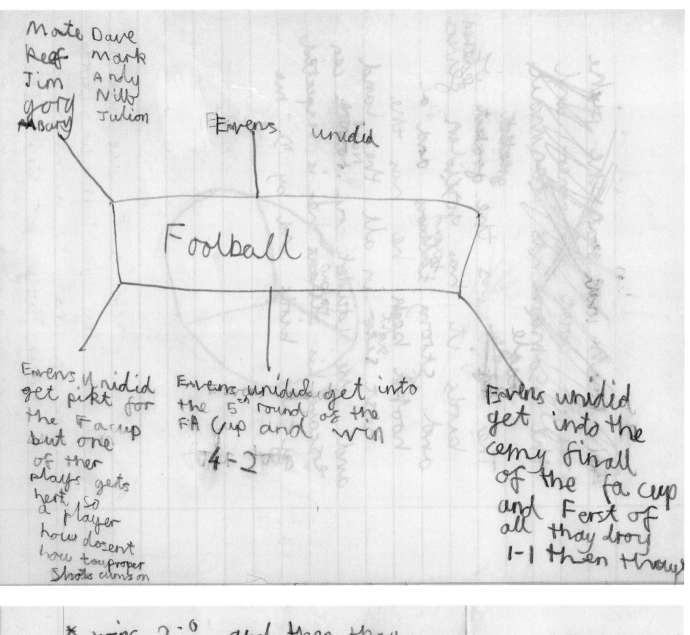

Mate Dave
Reef Mark
Jim Andy
Gory Nill
Bary Julion

Eevens unidid

Foolball

Eevens y nidid get pikt for the Facup but one of ther plays gets hert so a player how dosent how to proper shots cums on

Eevens unidid get into the 5th round of the FA Cup and win 4-2

Eevens unidid get into the cemy finall of the fa cup and ferst of all thay dror 1-1 then thay

* win 2-0, and then thay win the finall 3-2

53

The Eagle

The eagle is the gratest of birds it has goulden fevers and strong tallans and a hookt beak he has the best sight in all the land and the loudest cry. Nowone can escap his tallans he is respected by all birds and by me

School book aged 8

The eagle is the greatest of birds. It has golden feathers and strong talons and a hooked beak. He has the best sight in all the land, and the loudest cry. No one can escape his talons. He is respected by all birds and by me.

SET AS A POEM BY GEORGIE HAMMICK

The Eagle

The eagle is
The greatest of birds. It has
Golden feathers and strong talons
And a hooked beak. He has
The best sight in all the land, and
The loudest cry. No one
Can escape his talons.
He is respected by all birds
And by me.

The eagle is the gratest of
birds it has goulden fevers
and strong tallans and a
hookt beak he has the
best site in all the land
and the loudest cry. No wone can
escape his tallans he is resperted
by all birds and by my me

Wind

Oh wind you are so powerfull
You can be jentill and kind
But fers and mean
When you uprot trees and tos them into the
Air
You are the distroer of pece
And the killer of pece
You toss men into the ari as if
They were fevers
You are the gratist worier
That has ever been
With you grate
Strenth

Creative writing April 1996 aged 8

The teacher inserted the word 'happiness' thinking that probably when Johnnie showed it to her, he saw he had repeated 'peace' two lines running and wanted it changed.

Wind

O wind you are so powerful
You can be gentle and kind,
But fierce and mean
When you uproot trees
And toss them into the air.
You are the destroyer of peace
And the killer of happiness:
You toss men into the air as if
They were feathers.
You are the greatest warrior
That has ever been
With your great strength.

The Quiet River

As I walk down the bank I see
nachers beautiy with the
steam is making its sweat
song. The trees are a hundred
coulurs alone. The bank and
the strem has all the beauty
from the quiets mino to
loudes swallow. The birds songs are
more beatiful than the gratis
musisions. Oh to be with nacher.

School book 14 May 1996 aged 9

TRANSLATION SET AS A POEM

The Quiet River

As I walk down the bank I see
Nature's beauty with the stream making
Its sweet song. The trees
Are a hundred colours alone.
The bank and the stream
Have all the beauty from the quietest minnow
To the loudest swallow. The birds' songs are
More beautiful than the greatest musicians.
O to be with nature.

The Quiet River

Az I walk down the park I sel
nachers beauty with the
Steam is making its sweat
song. The trees are a hundred
coullbs alone. The bank and
the strem has all the beauty
from the quiets mino to
loudes Swallo. The birds songs are
more beatiful than the grah's
mulsisions. Oh to be with nacher.

The Morning Clowds

As I watch the beaeuty
Of the morning clowds
I see the scarlet
Within them, and
All the beauty the morning can give.
At the end of the clowds
Is a golden line with
The sun coming up
beaneth it.

15 November 1996 aged 9

The Fire

I watch the flams curel there fiery tungs
around the wood it makes me go into a wonderful
trance, that shuts me out of the world and makes
me fix my mind on the blazing fire.
The flames atack the wood and send it to join the
burning embers.

J.M.R. Douglas-Pennant
August 3rd 1997
aged 10

The Fox

He only comes out at night. He dosent ofden show himself but, when he dose he becomes ruler of the forest nothing dares attack him but he atacks the smaller and weeker animals. He has no mercy. He moves so quickly. He is like smoke one minet hes thair the next hes not he is the fox.

27 September 1997 aged 10

The Fox

He only comes out at night.
He doesn't often show himself
But when he does
He becomes ruler of the forest.
Nothing dares attack him,
But he attacks
The smaller and weaker animals.
He has no mercy
He moves so quickly
He is like smoke
One minute he's there
The next he's not
He is the fox.

The Fox

He only comes out at night.
He dosent ofden show himself but, when he dose
he becomes ruler of the forest nothing dares attack
him but he attacks the unsespecting chikens from the animal
He has no mercy   He moves so quikley He is
like smoke, one munet hes thair the next hes not
he is the fox

ANNA

As I long for her, only a mere memory
I wounder what would of happened if
the claw of death had not tacken her
God sent a rainbow at her death
I was not there to see her die
As she got thinner she tried in vain
to be active
She kept death out for fourteen
short years before she left her body
on earth and took her spirit to paridice
I could not believe it when she died for
I was only six and the lose of a loveing
sister was to much
I loved her then and I love her now

I can not take any praise for this poem

By Johnnie Douglas-Pennant

22 April 1998 aged 10

The first poem Johnnie wrote about Anna. It seems to have just come to him without him knowing how, which is why he put in the last line. He wrote it on the computer at school, and when I collected him that afternoon was carrying it in his hand ready to show me.

Johnnie aged 10 sitting reading on a rock in the hill loch in Jura where we scattered Anna's ashes and later his as well.

Gone

Gone far away,
Gone for good.
Gone a loved one,
Gone a light.
Gone to God,
Gone away from me.
Gone too early,
Gone too young.
Gone a soul,
Anna's gone.

Johnny Douglas-Pennant. 2.8.1998

Aged 11
This is the second poem about Anna, written when we were on holiday on the island of Jura.

Diana Heel, a healer friend and wise woman whom we first met when Anna was very ill wrote the following in response to Johnnie's poem 'Gone':

An Answer For Johnny

Anna has only gone from your sight
For now she walks in a body of light,
Open your heart and feel her near,
She has not gone, you have nothing to fear
Her soul has returned from whence it came
Her spirit flies free from stress and pain.
It is for your self you have to cry,
But know your angel is standing by.

Each have a destiny when we are born,
With very hard lessons we have to perform.
We all take part in creation's great plan,
Which is hard for us to understand.
Trust in God and say a prayer
Sending light and love for all to share;
With enough love nothing can sever
Each heart and each soul will abide forever.

Rainbow

She went after 14 years
She went on a rainbow
She went up to God
She travelled along that rainbow
She travelled with God
Her time was up
Her body motionless
She went to God
On heavens road

Sister

One of my sisters has gone now
She went at 14
My sister is in heaven now
My sister was a generator off love and affection
My sister was kind
My sister was good
My sister was loving caring and generous
My sister was an amazing mixture of every good thing
My sister was understanding
What more can I say, my sister was amazing
My sisters gone

Written together 8 October 1998 aged 11

Always

You could always be a friend
You could always listen to my problems
You were so un-belivably brave.
You always showed me the way
You always lightened the path, making it easy for me
to see,
You always were a rainbow one at your death
brought that to me.
You always were a rainbow as I said all the beautiful
Colours shown in your love all seven but in different way
of seven personalitys: love, care, attention, understanding,
fun, courage and something that I can't describe far to
emotional for words far too loving for words
Words would not give it due. It is far to
good for any word.

I loved her then I still love her but more
always

10 October 1998 aged 11

I have nevar seen a flower cry

I have nevar seen a flower cry
Or see a wild thing give up
but try and try again until they
have done what they set out to
do. Or see a animal feel sorry
for itself. I have nevar seen
a flower consider how
un-fair life is. I've nevar seen a
animal look scared or daunted.
So prehaps man should try to
bace part of his soul on a
animal. prehaps, but he nevar will

by J Douglas-Pennant 14.11.98

aged 11

I have never seen a flower cry
Or see a wild thing giveup
but try and try again until they
have done what they set out to
do. Or see a animal feel sorry
for itself. I have never seen
a flower ~~feel see~~ consider how
un-fair life is. I've never seen a
animal look scared or daunted.
So prehaps man should try to
base part of his soul on a
animal. prehaps but he never will

by J Douglas-Pennant 14.11.98

For a Fantastic Mum

Being a Mum isn't always fun
Some times there doesn't seem like there's any sun
Especially when your Port goes murky
And you make a balls up of the turkey
Or you catch me with tuck
And have to clear up the muck
Or maybe Dad gets home in a huff
Then makes you do all the boring stuff
And Mills does something bad
That makes you mad
No being a mum isn't always fun
But you're my number one.

Written for a Christmas present December 1998, aged 11

The children knew that when it came to presents I loved anything they had made. As Johnnie was not good with his hands he would usually write a poem. This explains why there are so many drawings and poems about me. I feel hesitant about including them but do so because they show the essential Johnnie.

If only I were! Drawn aged 10

Love (1)

It lives in the heart
It causes pain and happyness
It comes unexpectedly
And when it comes/you can't runaway from it
It may cause ~~much~~ unhappyness
Even death
But a year of unhappyness
Is worth a hour of it
It sets out to ~~dere~~ banish
All lonleyness

It changes peoples lives
Putting people emotions
On weighing scales
One minut there up
The next minut
There down/
It is love

Love (2)

I am everywhere
I'm lighter than air
I come unexpectedly
And when I come
You can't run away from me.
I send an arrow
Into the heart
Sometimes that arrow
Penetrates deep into the heart
Causing deep love.
I put your emotions
On weighing scales
One minute they're up
The next they're down
Creating unhappiness
But an hour of me
Is worth a year of lonliness.
I am love.

By JD-P

7 February 1999 aged 11. Second version of 'Love' written on the computer at school later the same day, which Johnnie decided at the time he didn't like. He might have changed his mind later.

You were there for me
You helped me through troubled times
You make my life
Whenether   I was covered in shadow you
Replaced it with light

You made me what I am
I would would put my heart, soul and life
I n your Hands
For I can trust you
I Love you, my wonderful Mum

Written by J D-P for S D-P on 23·6·99

The photograph shows JD-P and SD-P in 1994,
not long after Anna died. The poem opposite was
written as a 50th birthday present, aged 12.

Deep Sleep

Not dead just sleeping
She's just in a deep sleep

Don't make a sound
You might wake her
She deserves her sleep
After all the struggling,
the suffering and the trouble
She's been through She
need's a sleep
She'll wake up in a place
that is peacefull a place
That has no dieseas in it
She'll wake up in a place
called heaven

October 1999 aged 12

Deep Sleep

Not dead just sleeping
She's just in a deep sleep

Don't make a sound
You might wake her
~~Fake~~ She deserves her sleep
After all the struggling,
the suffering and the trouble
She's been through She
need's a sleep
She'll wake up in so a place
that is peacfull s a place
that has no dieseas in it
She'll wake up in a place
called heaven

A School Shooting

A school shooting
The murderer is now dead
Shott himself in the head

A mother searching the crowd of frightened children
Looking for her young boy
No sign of him

The socail worker is trying to comfort her
But she is determined he is not dead
'Her only joy has not gone' she hopes

Many relieved parents have children in their Arms
But hers is not among the alive

    She searches the building
    The classrooms
    The store cupboard
    The music room
    The gym
    No sign of him

But wait!
She hasn't searched the loos
She searches every cubical
She searches the last one
Theres a bean bag on the floor
She lifts it up
And underneath it
is her son

21 December 1999 aged 12

Thank You Mum

I owe alot to you, my mum
If I added it all up it would come to a tidy sum.
You've taken care of me since birth
And that hasn't always provided mirth.
Sometimes you must think my neck needs ringing
But you've overcome it by singing.
You've done all my dirty laundry
But that's only recently made me see
How wonderfall you are.

I've driven you mad,
I've made you sad.
For being a fantastic Mum
Thank you.

J Douglas-Pennant (Bompie Boy)
22·12·99 for
Mum

Poem about Granpa

Oh wonderful Grandpa
Why did you depart
And plunge us into sorrow
It seams when your
hapiness was at its
height God blew out the light
Your flowers will not want to bloom
Now that your in your tomb
You showed us how to grow old
Like a story being told
It could not have been better
The way you died
The way you lied, in your wifes arms
So grandpa I say a tearful farewell.

25 January 2000 aged 12

A few years after he was widowed Johnnie's Grandpa had remarried when already in his early eighties. He lived happily on until 90, and was a wonderful gardener. The poem was written in the pew waiting for the funeral service to start.

OPPOSITE *Christmas Card aged 12*

To Mum

You're family's not the easiest one
I'd say it's a lot harder than some
First their's me,
I'm surprised you didn't cry
When my results made it look like I didn't try.
Then theirs Milly,
You managed not to go into remourse
When she droped out of her University course.
And now that Dads a golfing bore
I'm sure he makes your ears sore.
You've put up with it all
You make us all feel very small.
We love you to bits

Jonks xxx

Birthday card, aged about 14

Happy Birthday Mum

Happy Birthday Mum, I hope you like your present.
I consider myself pretty impressive
Indeed I often make others jealous and aggressive

Through looks and charm
With the girls I can do no harm

I have brains and intelligence
As well as common sense

My conversation is so intresting
Society has simply named me the King

I owe this all to you my dear
Through love and guidence you've given me little to fear

You taught me the gift of the gab
And for that I think your just Fab

You made me confident and secure
So that I was never tempted by drugs as being 'something more'

And I love you for it.

Tongue-in-cheek birthday email, 24 June 2002 aged 15

Some weeks after this book was first published my nephew Edward arrived to stay. In the fifteen months since Johnnie had died I had resisted sorting his clothes but now we went upstairs to see if any of his shirts, new for his Work Experience, would fit Edward. Rummaging through another drawer afterwards, Edward lifted out some tee shirts. Hidden underneath them, right at the back, was another poem. It was written on a small piece of paper with the unused part of the page torn away so only the poem remained.

The Bird of Paradise

The bird of paradise deserves an eagle.
But has chosen a peacock.
For what?
For flashy appearance?
For multicoloured plumage?
For rank?
For false companions?
Can she not see through the exterior?
Can she not see the real eagles?
The eagles who don't appear so gorgeous or good
For what she surely does not know is some eagles
      come in a sparrow's body.

I imagine Johnnie would have been sixteen or so when he wrote this, and the fact that it seems to have come from the heart and may have been – who knows – about a girl, could have made him conceal it at the time.

Other Pieces

The Dragon of Fire

The bragonov fay wos a ver bab bragon hee bloby cusor an cotij – the kin sebi to nas a was to cil teh bragon – wen the knight sool The cuso won sab The fons knight the bragon bloo fay at the knit a he bad an t seco knight sh is sey an cib the bov fall sool the cuso won sab

Johnnie's first story that we have kept was almost incomprehensible to read but Milly was nearby at the time and added a translation as follows, writing underneath 'Johnnie made it up with NO help at all!'

TRANSLATION

The Dragon of Fire

The dragon of fire was a very bad dragon. He blowed up castles and cottages. The king sent two knights. He wants to kill the dragon. When the knight saw the castle he was sad. The first knight, the dragon blew fire at the knight and he died and the second knight charged with his spear and killed the dragon of fire.

Opposite below is Johnnie's illustration of his story.
January 1993 aged 5

The dragon [The dragon of fire]

The dragonov wose a VaserBab'bragon hee blob
Cusor one a n cotit
a wasThe Kin gebl to nas
to cineh by agon

wenThe knight
The fons Knit knight
The bragon BlOO
fay asThe knit
a he bad a n TSeco
knightsh with issey
an cib The bou fay

sOOlthe
cusowon
sab

Thecesac free ThebragonoV fay
← (the dragon of fire)

The to
knight

(the two knight's)

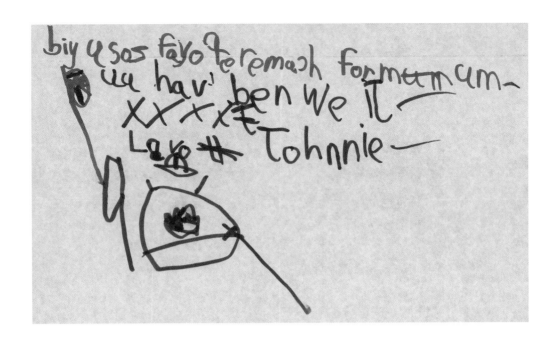

Dear Aunt Susie

biy u sos fayo fere mach for m um-
u u hav ben we it
xxxx
Love Johnnie

Dear Aunt Susie thank you very much for my
armour. I have been wearing it.
xxxx
Love Johnnie

January 1993 aged 5. Luckily Milly was there to translate!

Story in three chapters

chapter one

A island was in the sea a ship was in the sea at the same time I was on the ship with sum people. we were shipwrecled on the island only two peop survived one was me and the other one became my capyon I knew that the island looked like it was harmless but it was dangerous we made a boat and we tried to push it down to the sea it would not budge wen it got dark we were to tired so we lookt around there was no trees But there was a waterfall chapter two

insept from twe tree one was a banan tree and one was a
pawpaw I called get food and water I saw two crocodile as I
haf already mentuoned the island was dangerous we ran to a
secret hiding place in the waterfall the crocodile could not
find us in the waterfall wen he went away we got out of the
hiding place we got sum banan a then we made a fiye. This
was through nite in the morning we had a brakfast of waterfall water and banan and pawpaw and afte that we went
hunting

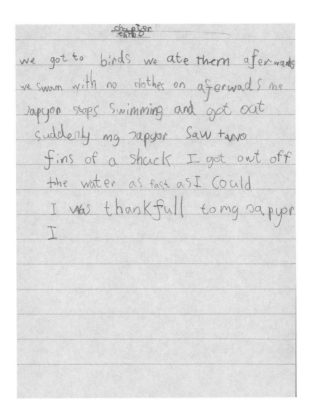

chapter three

we got to birds we ate them aferwards we swam with no clothes on aferwads me capyon stops swimming and got out suddenly my capyon saw two fins of a shuck I got out off the water as fast as I could I was thankfull to my capyon

capyon = companion   insept = except   twe = two
fiye = fire   shuck = shark

Undated, but writing looks aged 7. Looks as if there was someone nearby who helped with some of the spelling!

Invitation to an Asterix 8th Birthday Party

Dear
Plys cum to my Puty
cum as a Romon or one of the
gors don't all cum as gors becos
thel be no Romons to thump!
well I don't know about vat but vers
going to be a mag fit and dont cum as
Astriks bekos I am and don't
　　Love

Written in the car and unfortunately we arrived just then.

Dear
Please come to my party.
Come as a Roman or one of the
Gauls. Don't all come as Gauls because
there'll be no Romans to thump!
Well, I don't know about that there's
going to be a mega fight, and don't come
as Asterix because I am, and don't
    Love

Games and Guest List

1 Pin the tall on the wiyalld Boar
2 Punshing the Roman
3 Kicking the Roman

1 Jolyon 2 Louis 3 Achy 4 Berty 5 Chully
6 Alix 7 Ben 8 George M 9 Chris 10 James M
11 Daniel 12 Charlie D

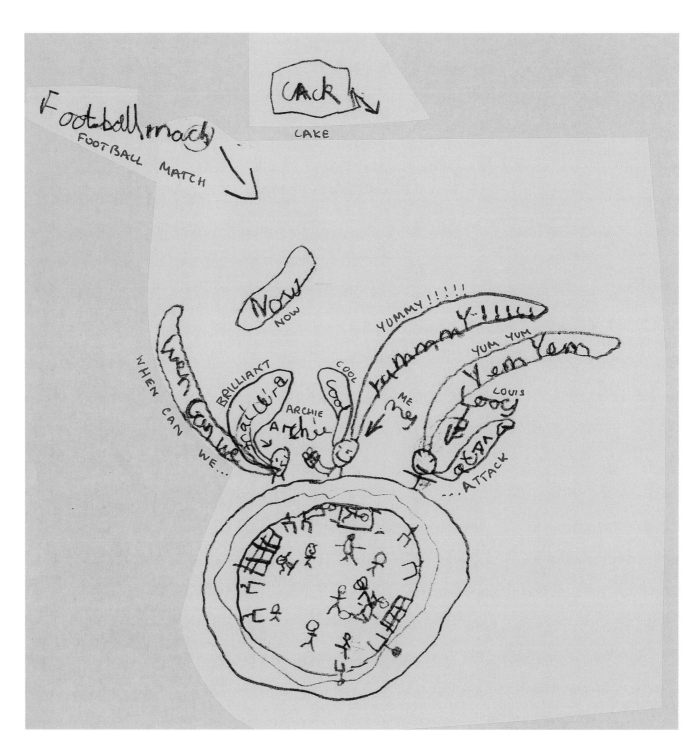

Design for cake (with translation!)

Food and Drink Plans

Food
1 Wild Boar Cake
2 cheese Bones
3 sausages
4 red cake with Yellow icing
5 chick legs

6 Green lemer ad

drinck
1 Ribena = wine
2 Green Lemer made =
Magic Potion

Johnnie cutting the 'wild boar' cake

Wish list of presents:

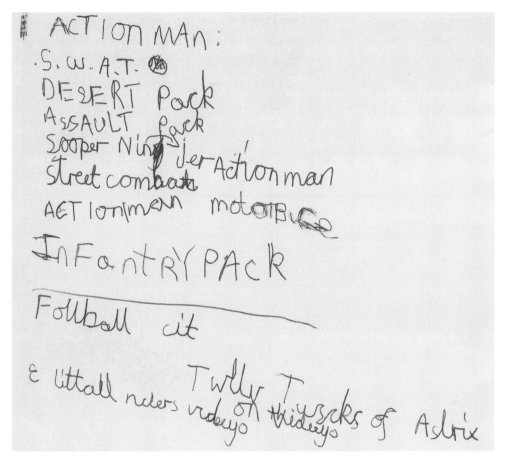

ACTION MAN	Follball cit
S.W.A.T.	Twllv Tuscks of Astrix on
DESERT Pack	videeyo
Assault Pack	3 littall nilers vedeeyo
Sooper Ninjer Action man	
Street Combat	*twllv=twelve*
Action man motor bice	*tuscks=tasks*
Infantry Pack	*nilers=??*

Johnny D-P MY

I live in Tisbry hous favret subgict is poetry and my spots
are Football and Rugby. wen am not at scool and my dads
not home I lisin to taps or rite poetry. I am 8 my siter's 41
my outher siter dide a year age wen she was 14. She did of
sitec fivebrosis wich is a un stoperball illnis that prevents
you from breving
      LICK ITS
      Flem   flem

                          Sis of her musal
                          Because of the illness

Dad Mum
    My   Mills

Johnny D-P   ME

I live in Tisbury House. Favourite subject is poetry and my sports
Football and Rugby. When (I) am not at school and my dad's not
home I listen to tapes or write poetry. I'm 8 my sister's 14 my other
sister died a year ago when she was 14. She died of cystic fibrosis
which is an unstoppable illness that prevents you from breathing.
LIKE ITS *(illustrated diagrams and picture of family)*:
    Phlegm   phlegm   size of her muscle
                              because of the illness
    Dad   Mum   Me   Mills

Johnny D-P **MY**

I live in Tisbry hous favret
Subgict is poetry and my spots
Football and Rengby. wen am not
at scool and my dads not hom
I lisin to taps or rite poetry.
Im 8 my siters 41 my outher
siter dide a year age wen she nas
14. She did of sitec-fivebrosis
wrchis a un sloper-ball illnis
that prevents you from brevirng.

LICK TIS

Fur   flem

sis of her musel

my   dad   mum   because
of the
illnis

milk

Letter to Paul who had just married our beloved Ally who had been nanny and school assistant with us for two years.

Dear Paul,   3rd October
     Whats it like being married to Aly? Hevon I suppose
Apurt from the Stuff like PAUL! brush uor hair NOW.
Wimin. Any way I loved the weding.
Our yes a nuver one
PAUL BRUSH you're her
Now. Send love to Aly from me.
         Love Jonks
             P.S.
             You handle
             Aly.

TRANSLATION

Dear Paul,
What's it like being married to Ally? Heaven I suppose. Apart from the stuff like PAUL! brush your hair NOW. Women. Anyway I loved the wedding.
Ah yes another one.
PAUL BRUSH your hair. Now. Send love to Ally from me.
Love Jonks
 P.S. You handle Ally

October 1995 aged 8

Port Regis,
Motcombe Park,
Shaftesbury,
Dorset. SP7 9QA

Dear Paul,,   3rd October
      Whats 'it like being
married to Aly? Hevon I suppose
apart from the the stuff like
PAUL 8 brush uor her NOW.
Wimin. Any way I Loved the weding.
Our yes   a niwer one
PAUL BRUSH your her
Now. Send Love to Aly from me.
    Love   Jonk's

       P.S
       You handle.
       Aly.

Dear Paul   28th November 95
     Whats the name of the place your living in now? I
exsect your alwass sneking out to the pub warst ally doing
 the washing up and when you get back your have to srub
the kichin flor. Hu tiperkol wimin hood hav am I serpos
yor lucky, you don't have are rotweiller in your house.
PR are giving soks and nicks to Bosneyer. Were doining
 a school play sory the D and E fors are doing a school play
 Im a monkey in it
          Love from
          Johnnie
           D and E forms are the two botom sets of forms.

TRANSLATION

Dear Paul
     What's the name of the place you're living in now? I expect
you're always sneaking out to the pub whilst Ally (is) doing the washing up and when you get back you have to scrub the kitchen floor.
How typical. Women. Who'd have 'em. I suppose you're lucky, you
don't have our rotweiller in your house. PR are giving socks and nicks
to Bosnia. We're doing a school play, sorry the D and E forms are
doing a school play. I'm a monkey in it.
          Love from Johnnie
               D and E forms are the two bottom sets of forms.

Aged 8

Dear Paul   2 8th November 95

whats the name of the
place your living in now? I
exsect your alwass Sneking out
to the pub warst ally doing
the woshing up and when you
get back your have to srub
the Kichis flor. Hu tiperkool
winin hood hav am I serpos
yor lucky, you dont have are
rotweiller in your house.
P R are giving soks and ricks to
Bocheyer. Were doining a school
play sory the D and Ɜ* fors are
doing a school play Im a
monkey in it

                 Love from
                 Johnie

                        * E D and Ɜ
              forms are the two
                        botom sets os

'Our rotweiller'

Dear father Christmas
     Please may I have
     a Southampton cap.
     a skill factor Alen shearer
     video.
     a Pro Action Football game

if there is such thing as some snap
football cards I'd like some of
those
and a southhamton scarf
a   reindeer hair band
a   toothbrush
a   southamton mug
a   suger mouse
and an orange
     thats all but can I please
have mainly things to do
with football.
     Love
     Johnnie Douglas - Pennant

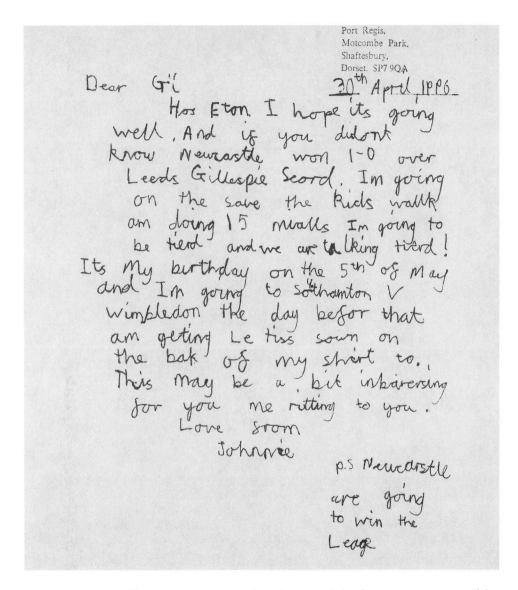

Port Regis,
Motcombe Park,
Shaftesbury,
Dorset. SP7 9QA

Dear Gi   30th April 1996

Hos Eton. I hope its going well. And if you didont know Newcastle won 1-0 over Leeds Gillespie Scord. Im going on the save the kids walk am doing 15 mealls Im going to be tierd and we are talking tierd! Its my birthday on the 5th of May and I'm going to Sothamton V wimbledon the day befor that am geting Le tiss sown on the bak of my shirt to. This may be a bit inbaversing for you me ritting to you.
         Love from
            Johnnie

            p.s Newcastle
            are going
            to win the
            Leage

Aged 8. Gi Milburn was 13 at the time and had just gone to public school. The friendship flourished in spite of the age difference, and it was Gi whose idea it was in the aftermath of Johnnie's death to walk with friends from Southampton to the Isle of Jura in his memory.

Letter offering money

A young matron at Johnnie's school was in tears one day because she had received a large telephone bill which she did not have the money to pay. Johnnie was moved by her distress and sent her the following note:

> Dear Iserbel,
>   I hope you have'nt paid the bill yet
> but if you'l take the money I'l
>   LEnd
>   £36.69
>   from
>   JOHNNY Douglas-Pennant

A letter came back in reply thanking Johnnie for his kind gesture, refusing the money, but saying how touched she was by his offer. October 1997 aged 10.

Essay

On a calm Christmas, snow is falling everybody is happy and reciving lots of presents A homeless, drugy and slightly acoholic teenager is shamberling along a city road looking for a doorway to sleep in, he looks in at the window and sighs everybody else is having a good time, how warm they looked he thought and the food looks so good, he sees some children with some left overs on there plate some brussel sprouts and some turkey and thinks I could eat that insted of giving it to dogs He then rembers christmas at his house he had been chucked out of his house when he was 16 his dad was a achollic and his mum couldent coup. He was 18 now He had only £70.00, 3 changes of clouths, a flick knife he used for mugging and thertning people, some bose and drugs, and a blanket. Now one loved him or even cared for him the nearest thing he'd had to that was a girl-friend who had left him a few months ago. He herd some church bells, something to do he thought so he went to church. When he got there the service was just starting he did'ent lisend to it very mutch but then they started to talk about people like him he lisend. At the end of the service he got one of the free bibles from the church. After that he gave up all drugs apart from fags and drunk boze modadrtey, got a job and raised enough mony to by a flat he got maried and had a family his job was talking to peo-ple who wanted to give up drugs

December 1997 aged 10   *coup = cope   Bose = booze*

Christmas thank you letter to Paul and Ally after they had had a son, Alex

Dear Alli and Paul (and Alex),
Thank you so much for the bath games and salts. They make bath time much more fun I had a bath yesterday and I tried every thing my favriots were the sharks teeth powder (it made the bath go green!) and the games. Hows Alli (this parts to Paul). Is she getting on your neves like: "Paul don't think I can't see you trying to get away to the pub, Im trying to bring up a family here, whats the child going to do if his dads never there always going to the pub getting drunk," or: "Paul do I have to do every thing here I clean your cloths, make your bed, cook your meals" ect. ect (after about 5 things she stops
She can't think anything else to say but she covers this up by saying: "the list is endless"). Sigh a bloke ca'nt get a minutes rest without wimin naging him WIMIN sigh wimin I will never understand, at least we now shes lovely really (not ha ha ha no I did'ent mean that when I said not). We spent Christmas in Irland. I hope you had a Happy Christmas and have a happy new year. Thanks again. See you soon

Love
Johnny

Now = know

29 December 1997 aged 10

Dear Alli and Paul (and Alex)...

Thank you so much for the bath games and salts. They make bath time much more fun. I had a bath yesterday and I tried every thing my favriots were the Sharks teeth powder (it made the bath go green!) and the games. Hows Alli (this parts to Paul) Is she getting on your neves like: "Paul I don't think I cant see you trying to get away to the pub, Im trying to bring-up a family here, Whats the child going to do if his dads never there, always going to the pub getting drunk", or "Paul do I have to do every thing here I clean your cloths, make your bed, cook your meals" ect. elt (after about 5 things she can't think anything else to say but she stops this up by saying: "the list is endless"). Sigh a bloke can't get a minutes rest with out wimin naging him WIMIN sigh wimin I will never understand, at least we now cover Shes lovely really (not ha ha ha no I didn't mean that when I did not). We spent Christmas in Irland. I hope you had a Happy Christmas and have a happy new year. Thanks again. See you soon

Love
Johnny

WEE ARE NOT AMUSED

Cystic Phibrosis

Cystic PPhibRosis is a quite common diseise. It is a diseise of the lungs. Various pills and machines have to be used for a pat any one who has it at home or at hospitel. Steroids and other pills have to be tacken at every meal. One of m My sister has Cystic Phibrosis and asthma asthma. Some of the equipment is a box with a tube comming out off it leading to a a thing shaped & like a gun witch the pat patient sticks in there mottth. My sister has Cf and one of my sisters died of it. X Sometimes my sister has to be on somthing called IVs wich is when she basicly has a x small hole in her arm with lots of tubes sticking out of it! Pauk Patients used to until very recently had to have something called piti pats this is when some- one sits next to a paitent who is lying down and consitently pats someone on there chest so they cough up a a sticky substance they spit into the Loo. Cystic fibrosis is not contagos so dont be afraid to kiss anyone who's got it.

May 1998 aged 11

'the equipment' described is a nebuliser for delivering vapourised drugs.
IVs = intravenous treatment. Piti pats = physiotherapy

'Mum, can I give you a bit of advice? When you get old
and a bit boring, and a bit bored of Dad,
DON'T TAKE UP SINGING!'

Johnnie chatting in the car aged 11

Family photograph taken two days before Johnnie died.

'If ever you need an escort, or a young soul to corrupt,
I'm your man.'

*From a letter to his octogenarian great aunt who had taken him
racing, and who he hoped would do so again. Aged 14.*

Johnnie and Dyspraxia

In this book I have included quite a few items of Johnnie's messy and poorly spelt work. At the time I remember despairing of his ever coming up to scratch with his written work. Even his drawings were desperately inept I thought. Yet looking at them now with their imaginative detail often acutely observed, and sensing the intelligence behind the written words, I wonder why I was so impatient with his lack of skill and facility. Parents of similarly struggling children should take heart that these difficulties to a large extent melt away as the child grows and develops. Other things that matter more come to the fore and the gaps in their abilities lessen as they overcome them or adapt.

Everyone has heard of dyslexia, which indicates difficulty with words. If a child has dyspraxia it means that their motor coordination is slow to develop, and they may have other hurdles to overcome as well, often including dyslexia. Typically they will be poor readers and writers, hopeless at things like cutting out or tying shoelaces, and regarded as no good at playground game or sports. It is very important to identify the problem early, and give appropriate exercises which can do much to improve coordination before the child realises he is doing 'exercises' or has lost confidence and become negative. Loss of self-esteem is all too easy when you are bad at everything young children want to be good at. During the early school years, the yawning gap between what the able child can do and what the dyspraxic child can becomes ever more marked, and it is very hard for them. The great challenge with these children is to keep their confidence up. The child needs understanding and appreciation of how much effort is required to master seemingly simple skills. It does all get easier as they get older. Their difficulties will one day have proved character-building which will stand them in good stead, and this is a heartening thing to remember when they are struggling. It is very tempting – I'm sure I was guilty – to direct all the focus on helping them overcome the things they find difficult, but it is just as important to look for things which they find fun and reasonably easy.

With Johnnie we did eye exercises, co-ordination exercises, re-educating the infant reflexes exercises, writing exercises etc etc and oh my goodness did it sometimes drive us nuts! Probably I fussed too much, as an ex-Montessori teacher, but we came through in the end. My heart bleeds for children who struggle without much support, suffering low marks in class and never being chosen to be in a team; these children are often very bright. It is not surprising if they become depressed or angry at experiencing so much failure. It is no coincidence that many young offenders have learning difficulties. This is a plea for sympathy, understanding and steady support for all dyspraxic sufferers, as well as for confidence that they will turn out just great in the end!

Afterword

Johnnie had started life exceptionally loving, bright and cheerful. By the time that he started writing the poems he had begun to find things more difficult. When he first went to school he gradually realised that aspects of scholastic life were going to be hard for him, and that he was also not well-coordinated for games, despite being as sports mad as any small boy. Soon after this he lost his sister, which further demoralised him. He struggled through those early years and was given various sorts of extra help both in and out of school, but it was not until he was eleven that we finally identified his difficulties as dyspraxia. By then he had had enough of well-intentioned people giving him yet another helpful exercise to perform, and refused to do any more. But he kept going in his own way, and kept trying to realise his abilities. As a friend had memorably once said, 'He needs to be cooked slowly.' She was right. Slowly but steadily his academic, social and sporting abilities improved.

His teachers had always said, 'Wait until he gets to A levels; then he'll really come into his own.' By the time he was seventeen his intelligence and understanding were coming to the fore and he was pulling away from the difficulties that had held him back. He did very well in his AS levels, receiving good marks in Economics, English and Philosophy, and an amazing 296/300 in History. At last he was proving himself and showing the world what he could do. He was due to join the Oxbridge class at school. He was looking forward to university.

It was at this point, to use his own phrase, that 'God blew out the light'.

I have a great belief that we are sent into this world for a particular purpose however short our lives might be. We have had to accept this hard fact of short lives in the case of two of our children and, like Wordsworth who lost his own son, can only be glad to have enjoyed them while we had them.

In the eternal scheme of things, the important consideration is not the length of a person's life. The only thing that matters has to be love, and a reading from Late Fragment by Raymond Carter which we had at Johnnie's funeral seemed to say it perfectly:

> And did you get what
> You wanted from this life, even so?
> I did.
> And what did you want?
> To call myself beloved, to feel myself
> Beloved on the earth.

Johnnie aged 16

I loved the Boy with the utmost love of which my soul is
capable, and he is taken from me – yet in the agony of my
spirit in surrendering such a treasure I feel a thousand
times richer than if I had never possessed it.

William Wordsworth